THIS BOOK BELONGS TO

_____

IN THE GARDEN

BY

CARALYN BUEHNER

ILLUSTRATED BY

BRANDON DORMAN

DESERET
BOOK

Library of Congress Cataloging-in-Publication Data

Buehner, Caralyn.
  In the garden / Caralyn Buehner ; illustrated by Brandon Dorman.
    p. cm.
  ISBN-13: 978-1-59038-403-9 (hardbound : alk. paper)
1. Holy Week—Juvenile literature. 2. Jesus Christ—Passion—Juvenile
literature. 3. Jesus Christ—Mormon interpretations—Juvenile literature.
4. Jesus Christ—Resurrection—Juvenile literature. I. Dorman, Brandon.
II. Title.
  BT414.B84 2007
  323.96—dc22   2006031833

Printed in the United States of America
Inland Graphics, Menomonee Falls, WI

10 9 8 7 6 5 4 3 2 1

For Mark, always

I KNOW THAT MY REDEEMER LIVES

—C.B.

Dedicated to my beautiful wife, Emily

—B.D.

In the evening before Jesus died, Jesus and his disciples met to eat the Passover meal. Jesus taught them to love and serve each other as he had loved them. He gave them the sacrament, and told them to remember his body and blood. He prayed for them, and promised to send the Holy Ghost to comfort them when he was gone.

He knew that it was time for him to suffer and die.

Just outside of Jerusalem was a garden, where Jesus often went, named Gethsemane. Jesus walked there with his disciples.

"Sit here," Jesus said, "while I go and pray."

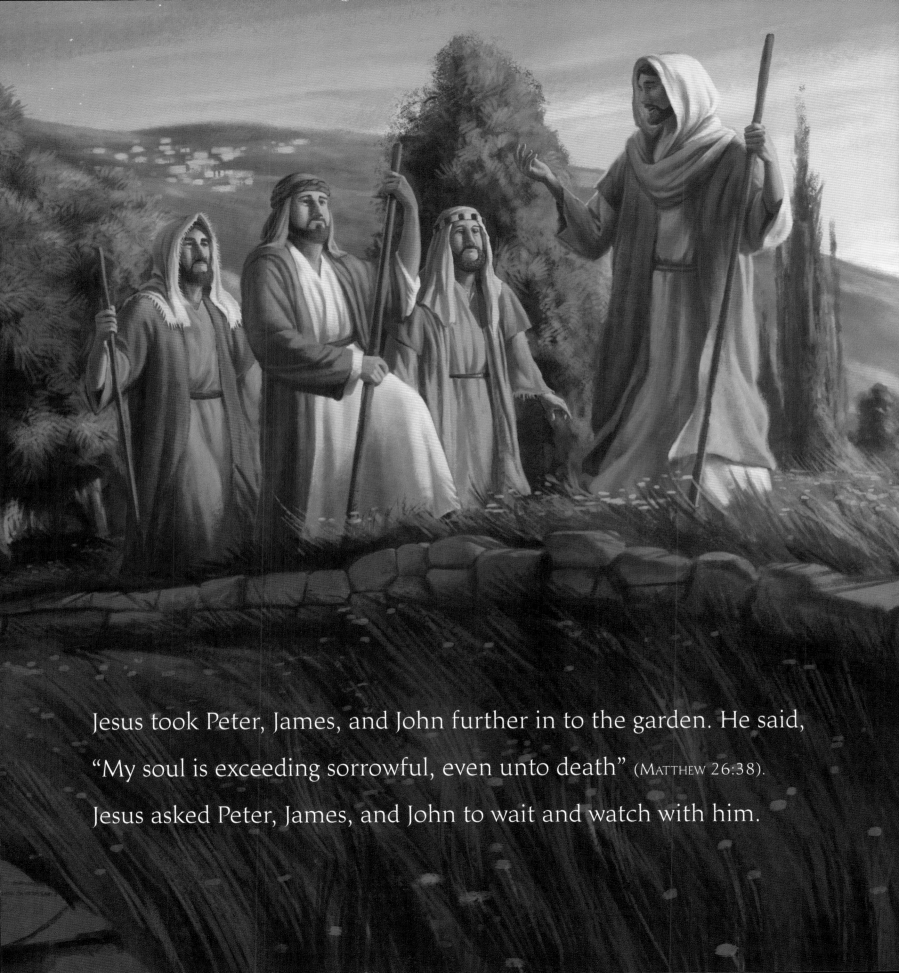

Jesus took Peter, James, and John further in to the garden. He said,

"My soul is exceeding sorrowful, even unto death" (MATTHEW 26:38).

Jesus asked Peter, James, and John to wait and watch with him.

Jesus prayed to Heavenly Father. He said, "Father, all things are possible unto thee; take away this cup from me: nevertheless, not what I will, but what thou wilt" (Mark 14:36).

Jesus was suffering. He was feeling all of the pain, hurt, anger, sickness, sorrow, weakness, and despair that anyone would ever feel, from the beginning to the end of time. It was part of Heavenly Father's plan that Jesus would suffer so that he would know perfectly how to help us.

But it was very hard.

J esus went back to where Peter, James, and John were sitting. They had fallen asleep.

Jesus woke them and asked them to pray.

Jesus prayed again. He asked that his suffering might be removed, if there was any way. But he also said, "Not my will, but thine be done" (LUKE 22:42). He was willing to do whatever his Heavenly Father needed him to do.

An angel came to strengthen him.

Jesus wanted his disciples to pray, but they were very sleepy. Jesus prayed with all his heart. He was in agony. He carried the weight of all the trouble in the world all by himself. He suffered more than anyone else ever would.

W hen Jesus went back to his disciples, he told them to rest. He said, "The hour is come; behold, the Son of man is betrayed into the hands of sinners" (MARK 14:41).

Jesus was taken by wicked men out of the garden. They took him to the Jewish leaders. Many of the Jewish leaders hated Jesus. He was laughed at, spit on, and beaten. People told lies about him.

The next morning Jesus was taken to the Roman leader, Pilate. Pilate knew that Jesus had done nothing wrong, and he was willing to let Jesus go. But the wicked men demanded that Jesus be killed.

Jesus was whipped, taken to Golgotha, and nailed to a wooden cross. Again he suffered as he had in the garden. He asked his disciple John to take care of his mother.

He prayed to Heavenly Father and asked forgiveness for those who crucified him. Then he gave up his life and died.

It was over.

The disciples of Jesus took his body down from the cross. They wrapped his body in linen cloths and placed it in a tomb. Everyone who loved Jesus was very sad.

Three days later, Jesus took up his body again and rose from his resting place. He appeared to his disciples. He let them feel the places in his hands and feet where the nails had been driven in.

The disciples were filled with joy!

Jesus lives today. Because of Jesus, we will live again, and if we repent, we will be forgiven of our sins. We will be able to live together forever with our families and with Heavenly Father and Jesus.

This is Heavenly Father's plan for us.

For God so loved the world, that he gave
his only begotten Son, that whosoever believeth in him
should not perish, but have everlasting life.

—JOHN 3:16